crafting*on*the*go

felt

crafting*on*the*go

felt

sixth&spring
books

sixth&spring
books

233 Spring Street
New York, NY 10013

Library of Congress Cataloging-in-Publication Data

Crafting on the go! Felt / [Editor, Trisha Malcolm]
    p. cm.
    ISBN 1-93154333X
    1. Felt work. I. Malcolm, Trisha, 1960- II. Crafting on the go!

TT880.C73 2003
    746'.0463--dc21   2002042942

Manufactured in China

1 3 5 7 9 10 8 6 4 2

First Edition

contents

introduction

Felt is one of the most versatile and practical craft fabrics available, which is why felt crafts are so popular with adults and children alike. Available in a virtual kaleidoscope of colors, felt is soft, durable and inexpensive. It's no surprise that over the years crafters have come up with an amazing array of applications for felt, from fashion accessories and embellishments to home decorating accents and beyond.

Forever a favorite, felt has existed for more than 8000 years with archaeological findings indicating the earliest use of felt in Turkey. In the Great Roman Empire, soldiers wore felted breastplates, tunics, boots and socks and in Scandinavia, records of felt use date back to the Iron Age. Today, felt is still used worldwide and continues to inspire modern crafters everywhere.

In this collection, stunning photographs and clear and concise instructions accompany each project. From fuzzy slippers to snazzy pillows, many of these easy-to-do projects are simple enough to craft with the kids. If you're looking to creating a special handmade gift from the heart, this must-have book is guaranteed to be a treasured addition to any crafter's library.

working with felt

Answers to the most common questions about creating with felt.

What is felt?

Felt is a non-woven matted fabric made when wool is subjected to moisture, heat and pressure. Once exposed to soap or an alkaline environment, the keratin of the wool fibers bind together chemically to create a permanent bond, which results in the tough and durable material.

How do I transfer a pattern to felt?

The easiest and most accurate way to transfer a pattern is to trace it onto freezer paper with the shiny side down. Iron the shiny side onto the felt, then cut out the pattern and peel off the paper.

Another option is to trace the pattern onto a piece of paper. Lightly coat the back of the paper with spray adhesive, allow it to dry, then press the paper onto the felt. Cut out the pattern and peel off the paper.

You can also trace the pattern onto paper, light cardboard or cardstock. Cut out the pattern, then tape or pin it to the felt and trace around the design using a disappearing-ink marker. Remove the pattern and cut out the design from the felt.

How do I mark a pattern directly onto a piece of felt?

Fabric-marking pens, especially disappearing-ink markers, work well on felt. Try different brands to see which you like best, and make sure to test them first on a scrap piece of the fabric. Colored pencils should be used only when the lines won't show on the finished project since the pigment may not brush away completely.

How do I cut felt?

Felt is easy to cut and won't ravel like woven fabric does. You can use fabric scissors and rotary cutters (including decorative-edge versions), as well as pinking shears and heavy-duty craft punches.

What glues should I use?

Before tackling any felt project, protect your work surface and test the adhesives to be sure of their results. Thick craft glue works well for most basic projects. (Thin glues will soak into the felt.) Fabric glues, such as Fabri-Tac™ by Beacon™, are also effective, and most brands are washable. (Make sure to check the manufacturer's guidelines before washing.) Gem-Tac™ by Beacon™ is a good choice for attaching sequins, rhinestones and beads, while hot glue works well for attaching larger embellishments, such as pin backings and silk flowers.

Fusible web, which irons on easily, is ideal for applying appliqués. However, felt can also be sewn by hand or machine. For items that don't need to be stitched, sheet adhesives can be used.

(for one bag)

- **Kunin Rainbow Classic Felt™: four 9" x 12" (22.9cm x 30.5cm) pieces (three in main color and one in contrasting color)**

- **Other supplies: sewing machine, sewing needle, contrasting-color sewing thread, straight pins, scissors, pinking shears (optional), graph paper, pencil, ruler**

in the bag

Reusable felt sacks make an interesting (and eco-friendly) alternative to traditional boxes and wrapping paper. A simple loop closure secures the opening.

1 On graph paper, draw one 6½" x 9" (16.3cm x 22.9cm) rectangle (for front and back of bag), one 3½" x 9" (8.8cm x 22.9cm) rectangle (for sides) and one 3½" x 6½" (8.8cm x 16.3cm) rectangle (for bottom). Cut out. Using patterns, cut out front and back, two sides and one bottom from main color felt. (Optional: Cut along top edges of front, back and sides using pinking shears.) For tie, cut a ¾" x 12" (1.9cm x 30.5cm) strip from contrasting-color felt.

2 With wrong sides facing, pin front and back to sides. Beginning at top edge, topstitch seam ¼" (.6cm) from edge to within ¼" (.6cm) of bottom edge.

3 Pin bottom to front, back and sides. Beginning ¼" (.6cm) from corner, topstitch seam ¼" (.6cm) from edge to within ¼" (.6cm) of next corner. Repeat across next three sides.

4 On front and back, cut a ¾" (1.9cm)-wide horizontal slit ¾" (1.9cm) from top edge and centered side to side.

5 Draw tie through slits and make a single overhand knot. Cut ends of tie at an angle to desired length.

Stars

- Kunin Rainbow Classic Felt™: one 3" x 5" (7.6cm x 12.7cm) piece each Yellow and Crystal Blue

Fish

- Kunin Rainbow Classic Felt™: one 3" x 5" (7.6cm x 12.7cm) piece Lavender and one 2" x 3" (5cm x 7.6cm) piece each Yellow and Crystal Blue

- One 3" x 5" (7.6cm x 12.7cm) piece Pellon® Wonder-Under® paper-backed fusible web for each motif

- Six-strand embroidery floss in bright orange-yellow, bright turquoise and lime

- Purchased infant onesie and hat

- Other supplies: pencil, scissors, iron, ironing board, embroidery needle

shower stars

Is there a little one on the way? Personalize newborn essentials like caps and onesies with tiny star and fish appliqués.

1 Trace star and fish patterns onto the paper-side of the fusible web.

2 Following the manufacturer's directions, fuse the web to the wrong side of the felt color listed and carefully cut them out. Remove the paper and fuse as directed to the right side of the backing felt, leaving space in between the motifs. (Note: The backing felt should remain whole at this point.)

Stars

3 Using two strands of orange-yellow floss, whipstitch the large Yellow star to the Crystal Blue felt. Using one strand of orange-yellow floss, whipstitch the small Crystal Blue star to the Yellow felt.

templates

**Templates are
actual size.**

**Cut one large star
from Yellow felt.**

**Cut one small star
from Crystal Blue felt.**

**Cut one large fish
from Lavender felt.**

**Cut one small fish
from Yellow felt.**

Fish

4 Using two strands of lime floss, whipstitch each
large Lavender fish to the Peacock felt. Use two
strands of lime floss and a double-wrapped
French knot to create an eye. Using one strand of
turquoise floss, whipstitch each small Yellow fish
to the Lavender felt. Use two strands of turquoise
floss and a double-wrapped French knot to
create an eye.

5 Following the manufacturer's directions, fuse
the web to the wrong side of the backing felt.
Carefully cut the backing felt around each motif,
leaving a ⅛" (.3cm)-wide edge showing.

6 Remove the paper backing from the motifs.
Referring to the photo for placement, fuse the
stitched appliqués into position on the onesie
and hat.

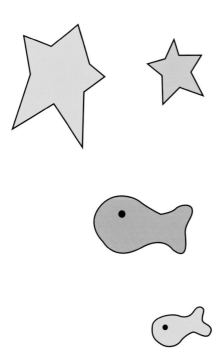

head start

Kunin Rainbow Classic
Felt™: remnants in Leaf
Green, Ruby, Plum and
Deep Rose

3" (7.6cm) metal
hair barrette

Six-strand embroidery
floss in cranberry,
yellow and pink

Other supplies:
disappearing-ink
marker, pinking shears,
needle, hot-glue gun
and glue sticks, thick
craft glue, scissors

**Tuck an ever-fresh flower into your tresses.
This pretty posie design can be glued
to a barrette, headband or ponytail holder.**

1 Trace the leaf pattern onto Leaf Green felt and
cut out with pinking shears. Using two strands of
yellow embroidery floss, topstitch around the leaf
edges. Center the leaf on the barrette and attach
with hot glue.

2 Trace the large flower pattern onto Ruby felt and
the small flower onto Deep Rose felt; cut out.
Blanket-stitch around the petals of the small
flower using two strands of cranberry embroidery
floss. Place the small flower on top of the large
flower and secure them with a dot of glue.
Loosely wrap two strands each of cranberry,
yellow and pink floss around your finger four
times; tie in the middle and attach to the center
of the flower with a dot of glue. Cut the loops
and trim floss as pictured.

3 Trace four side petals onto Plum felt and cut out.
With yellow embroidery floss, tie two petals
together at their centers to create a flower shape.
Trim floss, leaving approximately ½" (1.3cm) of
fringe. Repeat with the two remaining petals.

4 Center and hot-glue the large flower to the top of the leaf. Hot-glue the side petals to the leaf on each side of the large flower.

Templates are actual size.

Cut one leaf from Leaf Green felt.

Cut one large flower from Ruby felt.

Cut one small flower from Deep Rose felt.

Cut four side petals from Plum felt.

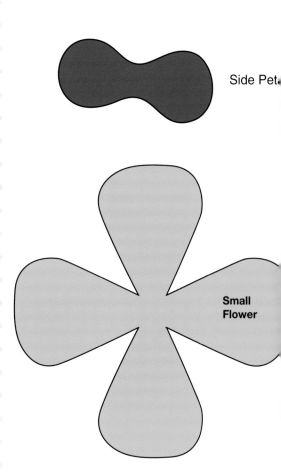

Side Petal

Small Flower

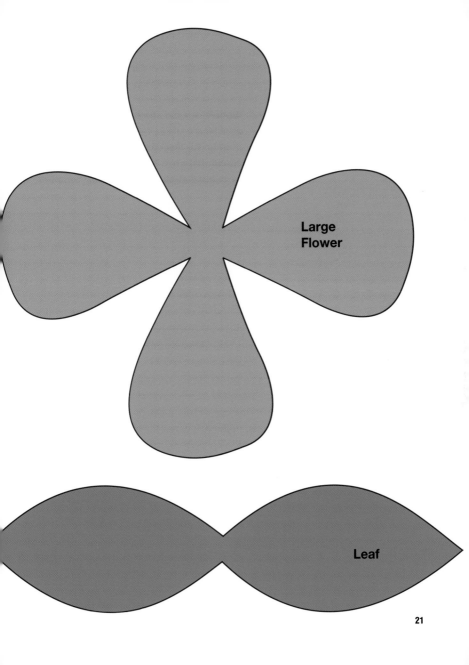

Large Flower

Leaf

- **Kunin Glitter Felt™: ¼yd (.23m) Red and ¼yd (.23m) White**

- **Six-strand embroidery floss in red**

- **Other supplies: scissors, embroidery needle, thick craft glue, hot-glue gun and glue sticks or double-sided tape**

heart to heart

Show a special someone that you care by attaching a "heart-felt" tag to a gift of love. Perfect for Valentine's Day, simply cut out gradating-size hearts in alternating colors, trim with blanket-stitch and hot-glue together.

1 Photocopy large, medium and small heart; cut out. Using the templates, cut hearts from the felt colors listed.

2 Adhere the large White and Red hearts using small dots of glue; let dry. With two strands of embroidery floss in the needle, blanket-stitch around the hearts. Blanket-stitch around the medium Red heart and the small White heart in the same manner.

3 Layer hearts on top of one another from largest to smallest, adhering them with small dots of glue. Attach the heart to a gift using a dot of hot glue or a small square of double-sided tape.

Variation

Photocopy top and backing hearts and cut out.
Using the templates, cut one backing heart from
Red felt and one top heart from White felt. Layer
the White heart on top of the Red heart. Using a
long stitch length and red embroidery floss, stitch
around the White heart ¼" (.6cm) in from the
outer edge.

**Templates are
actual size.**

**Cut one large heart
from Red felt.**

**Cut one large heart
from White felt.**

**Cut one medium
heart from Red felt.**

**Cut one small heart
from White felt.**

Variation

**Cut one backing
heart from Red felt.**

**Cut one top heart
from White felt.**

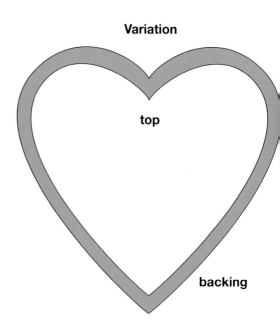

Variation

top

backing

Large Heart

medium

small

- **Kunin Rainbow Classic Felt™: 1yd (.92m) Peacock, one 9" x 12" (22.9cm x 30.5cm) piece each Lime, Orange, Lavender, Baby Blue, White, Purple, Aqua, Yellow, Red, Pink Punch, Coffee and Soft Beige**

- **Other supplies: disappearing-ink marker, scissors, craft glue**

under the sea

Colorful ocean creatures cut from colorful felt swim happily in an easy-to-assemble aquarium. Makes a great accent: for a playroom or kids' bath.

1 Photocopy the templates and cut them out. Using the templates, cut the shapes from the felt colors listed.

2 Cut a 36"x 40"(90cm x 100cm) piece of Peacock felt for the background.

3 Cut out the fish eyes and shell accents from the felt colors indicated by the photo and glue them in place. Arrange the on the Peacock felt background as desired.

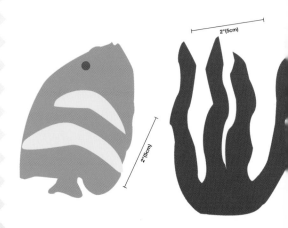

templates

Cut the sand from Soft Beige felt.

Cut two rocks from Coffee felt.

Cut the plant from Lime felt.

Cut six sets of bubbles from White felt.

Cut the starfish from Orange felt.

Cut the octopus from Aqua felt.

Cut the crab from Red felt.

Cut the sea horse, dolphin and waves from Baby Blue felt.

Cut the shells and fish from Orange, Pink Punch, Purple, Lavender, Yellow, Aqua, Baby Blue and White as indicated in the photo.

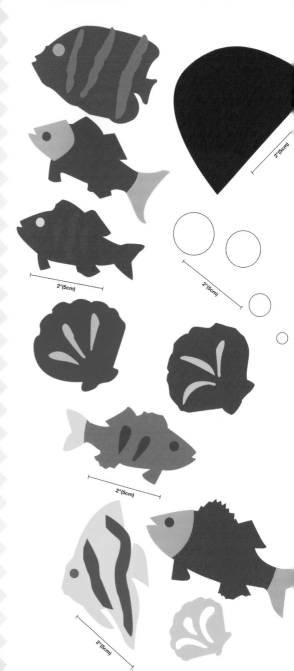

2"(5cm)

2"(5cm)

2"(5cm)

2"(5cm)

2"(5cm)

2"(5cm)

2"(5cm)

36"(90cm)

baby blocks

Soft stuffed felt blocks make a fitting first gift for baby. Use the letter appliqués with a heart for V to spell out baby and love.

- **Kunin Rainbow Classic Felt™: seven 9" x 12" (22.9 cm x 30.5 cm) pieces (one White, three Neon Blue and three Yellow)**

- **4" (10.2cm) and 3" (7.6cm) square templates**

- **Fiskars® Softgrip® Scallop Fabric Scissors**

- **1yd (.92m) iron-on interfacing**

- **9" x 12" (22.9cm x 30.5cm) piece fusible web**

- **12 oz. bag polyester fiberfill**

- **Other supplies: disappearing-ink marker, pencil, scissors, iron, ironing board, straight pins, sewing needle, sewing machine, matching thread**

1 Trace twelve 4" (10.2cm) squares each onto Neon Blue and Yellow felt, leaving a small space between each square. Cut out along lines using scallop scissors.

2 Cut 24 3" (7.6cm) squares from interfacing. Center and iron one interfacing square onto each felt square.

3 Fuse web to White felt following manufacturer's instructions.

4 Cut out letters, remove paper and fuse letters to centers of four Neon Blue and four Yellow squares, beginning with the letters B and L on Neon Blue. Alternate background colors for remaining letters.

5 Pin four plain Neon Blue squares together into a tube to form an open-ended block. Topstitch each side ¼" (.6cm) from the edge.

6 Pin Yellow squares to ends and stitch. Leave a small opening in the center of one side for stuffing. Clip all threads. Stuff blocks, pushing fiberfill into corners first. Topstitch openings shut. Repeat for all four blocks, alternating colors.

templates

Templates are actual size.

Cut two B's and one of each of the other letters from White felt.

Cut one heart from White felt.

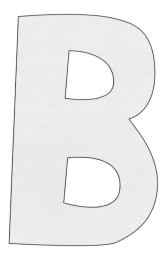

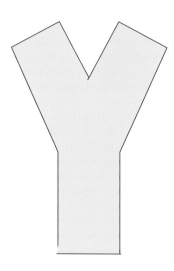

33

materials

Star

Kunin Rainbow Classic Felt™: ⅔yd (.61m) Grape and remnants in Apple Green, Light Yellow, Deep Rose, Baby Blue and Pink Punch

⅔yd (.61m) iron-on interfacing

Six-strand embroidery floss in red

Moon

Kunin Rainbow Classic Felt™: ½yd (.46m) Aqua and remnants in Light Yellow, Deep Rose and Baby Blue

½yd (.46m) iron-on interfacing

Six-strand embroidery floss in yellow

Both pillows

12 oz. bag of polyester fiberfill

Other supplies: disappearing-ink marker, scissors, iron, ironing board, straight pins, sewing machine, sewing needle, matching thread

starry nights

Encourage sweet dreams with just-for-fun pillows crafted in moon and star shapes. Perfect for a teen's room!

Star

1 Trace two stars onto Grape felt; cut out. Cut two 2" x 30" (5cm x 76.2cm) strips from Grape felt.

2 Following the manufacturer's directions, fuse interfacing to the backs of the stars and the strips.

3 Sew the strips together at the end using a ½" (1.3cm) seam.

4 Line up the strip seam with the center point of one star at the top. Pin the strip around the star so the second seam is lined up with the center-bottom of the star. Sew the second strip seam, trimming off any excess.

5 Sew the strip to the star, right sides together, with a ½" (1.3cm) seam. Repeat for the second star piece, leaving an opening at the bottom.

6 Cut one swirl each from Apple Green, Light Yellow, Baby Blue and Pink Punch felt. Position the swirls on pillow top as desired and sew on with running stitch.

7 Using two strands of red floss, embroider French knots, evenly spaced, around edge of pillow top.

templates

Star

Cut two stars from Grape felt.

Cut one swirl each from Apple Green, Light Yellow, Deep Rose, Baby Blue and Pink Punch.

Moon

Cut two moons from Aqua felt.

Cut one swirl each from Light Yellow, Deep Rose and Baby Blue.

8 Clip the seam allowance around all curves and carefully turn pillow right side out.

9 Stuff star with fiberfill, beginning with the points. Slipstitch opening shut.

Moon

1 Trace two moons onto Aqua felt; cut out. Cut one 2" x 33" (5cm x 83.8cm) and one 2" x 17" (5cm x 43.2cm) strip from Aqua felt.

2 Following the manufacturer's directions, fuse interfacing to the backs of the moons and the strips.

3 Sew the strips together at the end using a ½" (1.3cm) seam.

4 Line up the strip seam with the center point at the top of one moon piece. Pin the strip around the moon so the second seam is lined up with the center-bottom point of the moon. Pin and sew the second strip seam, trimming off any excess.

5 Sew the strip to the moon, right sides together, using a ½" (1.3cm) seam. Repeat with the second moon piece, leaving an opening at the bottom.

6 Cut one swirl each from Light Yellow, Deep Rose and Baby Blue felt. Position swirls on pillow top as desired and sew on with running stitch.

7 Using two strands of yellow floss, embroider French knots, evenly spaced, around edge of pillow top.

8 Clip the seam allowance around all curves and carefully turn pillow right side out.

9 Stuff moon with fiberfill, beginning with the points. Slipstitch opening shut.

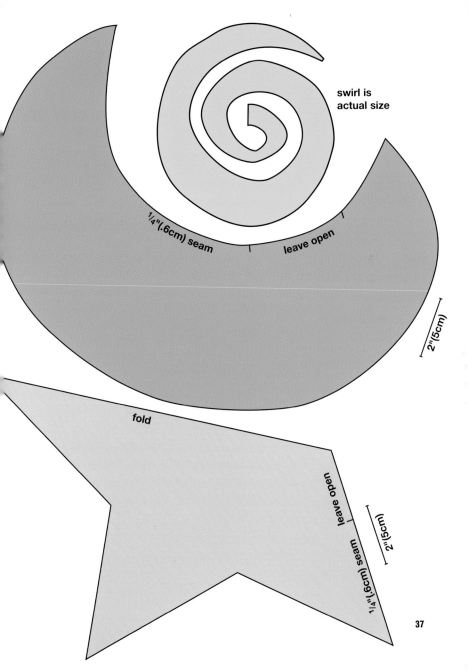

swirl is
actual size

¼"(.6cm) seam

leave open

2"(5cm)

fold

leave open

2"(5cm)

¼"(.6cm) seam

37

- Kunin Rainbow Classic Felt™: five 9" x 12" (22.9cm x 30.5cm) pieces (three Pumpkin, one Cinnamon and one Hunter Green)

- 6" (15.2cm) Styrofoam™ ball

- 4" x 20" (10.2cm x 50.8cm) piece of polyester quilt batting

- 18" (45.7cm) of copper wire

- Beacon™ Fabri-Tac™ glue

- Six-strand embroidery floss in brown

- Other supplies: craft knife and cutting mat, straight pins, sewing needle, sewing machine, matching thread, pencil, scissors, wire cutters

harvest time

Welcome fall with a perfectly padded pumpkin. Group several near the doorway for a festive autumn accent or on the table for a great centerpiece.

1 Using the craft knife, cut a thin slice off one side of the Styrofoam™ ball to create the bottom of the pumpkin.

2 Wrap the ball in two layers of quilt batting.

3 Using ½"(1.3cm) seams, sew two pieces of Pumpkin felt together along the 9" (22.9cm) sides to create a tube. Run a basting stitch around the top and bottom openings. Leave the threads hanging.

4 Slide the felt tube over the pumpkin ball. Pull the basting stitches tight at the top and bottom. Secure the threads.

5 Knot six strands of floss together and secure with a knot at the pumpkin top. Bring the floss down along the seam line, wrapping it firmly around the entire pumpkin and pulling it back up to the top again. Sew one stitch to secure the floss at the top. Repeat, wrapping the pumpkin along the opposite halfway marks, then in halves again. Secure at the top and clip threads.

6 Trace the pumpkin top onto Cinnamon felt and cut out. Glue it in place.

7 Cut a ½" x 5" (3.8cm x 12.7cm) strip from Cinnamon felt for the stem. Wrap into a tight tube and glue to secure. Glue the stem to the pumpkin top as pictured.

8 Trace four leaves onto Hunter Green felt and cut out. Topstitch pairs of leaves together, leaving an opening at one end for the wire stem.

9 Cut two 5" (12.7cm) pieces of copper wire and insert them into the open centers of the leaves. Bend the leaves slightly. Wrap the wire ends around the stem. Curl both ends of the remaining wire around a pencil four or five times. Wind the center of the wire around the pumpkin stem to secure.

templates

Cut four leaves from Hunter Green felt.

Cut one pumpkin top from Cinnamon felt.

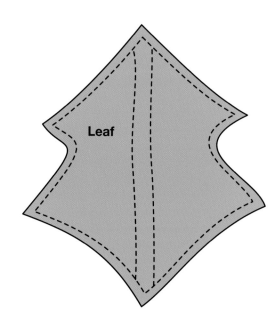

Leaf

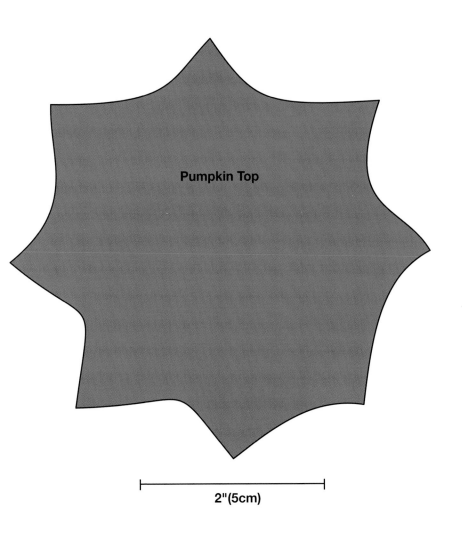

Pumpkin Top

2"(5cm)

- **Kunin FlashFelt™:
  four 9" x 12" (22.9cm x
  30.5cm) pieces (three
  SnowFelt White and one
  Deep Space Black)**

- **Kunin Glitter Felt™:
  one 9" x 12" (22.9cm x
  30.5cm) piece Purple**

- **One 5" (12.7cm) and
  one 3" (7.6cm)
  Styrofoam™ ball**

- **One 3⅜" x 4⅞" (8.6cm x
  12.4cm) Styrofoam™ egg**

- **Beacon™ Fabri-Tac™
  glue**

- **⅓yd (.31m) polyester
  quilt batting**

- **One ¾" (1.9cm) red and
  three ½" (1.3cm)
  assorted-color buttons**

- **Two ⅛" (.8cm) black
  safety eyes**

- **5"(12.7cm), 2¼"(5.7cm)
  and 2" (5cm) circle
  templates**

- **½yd (.46m) medium
  rickrack in red**

- **Other supplies:
  craft knife and cutting
  mat, straight pins, sewing
  needle, sewing
  machine, matching
  thread, scissors,
  fabric marking pencils,
  pinking shears**

frosty snowman

**Craft this adorable snowman and add cheery
details like a hat, scarf and buttons to make him
come to life. Place him on a mantle,
in the kitchen or den, and feel winter's magic.**

1 Using the craft knife, cut thin slices off opposite
sides of the 5" (12.7cm) ball. Cut a thin slice from
one side of the 3" (7.6cm) ball. Cut one third off
the narrow end of the egg and a thin slice off the
large end.

2 Glue the cut narrow end of the egg to one cut
side of the 5" (12.7cm) ball. Glue the cut side of
the 3" (7.6cm) ball to the other end of the egg.
This will create the snowman shape.

3 Wrap the snowman with two layers of
quilt batting.

4 Sew two SnowFelt White pieces together along
the 12" (30.5cm) sides and turn inside out to
create a tube. Baste around the top and bottom
openings, leaving the threads hanging.

5 Slide the felt tube over the snowman form.
Pull the basting stitches tight at top and bottom.
There will be a small opening on each end.

6 Cut a 2" (5cm) circle from SnowFelt White.
Glue over the bottom opening of the snowman.

7 From Purple felt, cut two 2" x 10" (5cm x 25.4cm)
strips for a scarf and one 1" x 8¼" (2.5cm x
20.9cm) strip for a hat band.

**Cut two snowman
patterns from
SnowFelt White.**

8 Glue two ends of the scarf strips together and make fringe by cutting in from each loose end about 1½" (3.8cm) with pinking shears. Cut two 2"(5cm) pieces of rickrack and glue across scarf ends just above fringe. Tie the scarf around the snowman's neck where the 3" (7.6cm) ball joins the egg. Glue in place. Glue the large red button to the scarf as pictured.

9 Use the sharp point of a pair of scissors to make holes for eyes in the center of the face. Insert the ends of the safety eyes into the holes and glue in place.

10 Glue other buttons down the front of the snowman.

11 Cut one 5" (12.7cm) circle, one 2¼" (5.7cm) circle and one 2" x 8" (5cm x 20.3cm) band from Deep Space Black felt.

12 Glue the band ends together to create a tube. Glue the 2¼" (5.7cm) circle to the end of the tube to create the hat top.

13 Cut a 1⅞" x 12" (4.7cm x 30.5cm) strip of quilt batting. Roll and insert into the hat top to keep its shape.

14 Place dots of glue around the inside bottom edge of the hat top. Center the top on the 5" (12.7cm) black circle and finger-press in place.

15 Glue the Purple felt hatband strip around the hat. Cut two 8¼"(20.9cm) pieces of rickrack and glue around top and bottom of hat band.

16 Glue the hat to the snowman's head, covering the small opening.

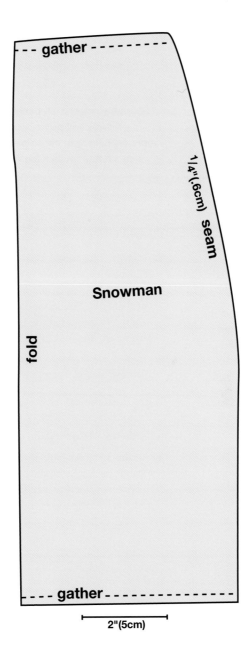

gather

$^1/_4"$(.6cm) seam

Snowman

fold

gather

2"(5cm)

(for one party hat)

- **Kunin Rainbow™ Classic Felt: one 9" x 12" (22.9cm x 30.5cm) piece Pink Punch, one ½" x 24" (1.8cm x 61cm) strip each Pink Punch, Lime and Yellow, one ½" x 12" (1.3cm x 30.5cm) strip each Pink Punch, Lime and Yellow, remnants of Grape, Pink Punch, Yellow, Lime, Peacock and Orange**

- **One 9" x 12" (22.9cm x 30.5cm) piece paper-backed fusible web**

- **Other supplies: disappearing-ink marker, scissors, iron, ironing board, sewing machine, sewing needle, matching thread, embroidery needle**

party time

Vibrantly colored felt party hats trimmed with tassels and polka dots are so much more enticing than the store-bought variety. Have kids craft them as a fun-filled party activity.

1 Trace the hat pattern onto the Pink Punch felt and cut out.

2 Following the manufacturer's instructions, back the small felt remnants with fusible web. Draw dots onto the paper side of the fusible web and cut them out. Position the dots on the hat piece, keeping in mind that the brim will cover the lower part, and fuse in place.

3 Stitch the two straight sides of the hat together, right sides facing, and turn right side out.

4 Flat-braid the three 24" (61cm) strips of felt. Pin to the bottom edge of the hat and hand stitch to create a brim.

5 Cut the 12" (30.5cm) felt strips into four 3" (7.6cm) pieces. Stack the colors and, using heavy embroidery thread, tie in the middle and stitch to the top of the hat.

(for one party hat)

Copy to size and match up two pieces to form one template.

Cut one party hat from Pink Punch felt.

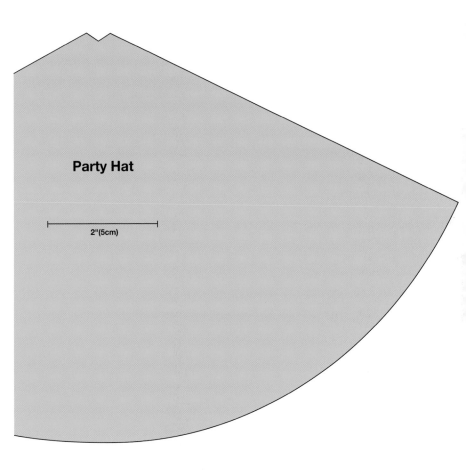

Party Hat

2"(5cm)

(for one placemat)

- Kunin Rainbow Classic
  Felt™ : two 6" x 8"
  (15.2cm x 20.3cm) pieces
  each Antique Gold and
  Ruby, one 5" (12.cm)
  square each Pumpkin
  and Walnut Brown, ½yd
  (.46m) Soft Beige

- ¾yd (.69m) fusible web

- Other supplies:
  ruler, scissors, iron,
  ironing board, sewing
  machine, sewing needle,
  matching thread,
  pinking shears or
  scallop-edge scissors

make the meal

**Easy-to-make felt placemats add an elegant air
to the table. The leaf appliqué shown here
is perfect for the harvest season. Opt for a star
or tree for holiday décor, a fish or sailboat for
summer dining.**

1 Cut a 12¾" x 16½" (32.4cm x 41.3cm) rectangle
from the Soft Beige felt for the placemat backing.

2 Iron fusible web onto the Antique Gold and
Ruby rectangles, following the manufacturer's
directions. Position the four pieces evenly on
the backing, leaving a small Soft Beige border
visible around the placemat; iron to bond.

3 Iron fusible web onto the Pumpkin felt and the
remaining Soft Beige and Walnut Brown pieces.
Trace the leaf pattern onto the Pumpkin and
Soft Beige felt and cut out. Position the leaves
in the corners of the placemat and iron to bond.

4 Trace the leaf vein pattern twice onto the Walnut
Brown felt. Cut the veins out carefully, place on
the leaves and iron to bond.

5 Topstitch around the placemat and trim
the Soft Beige edges with pinking shears or
scallop-edge scissors.

(for one placemat)

Templates are actual size.

Cut one leaf from Pumpkin felt.

Cut one leaf from Soft Beige felt.

Cut two leaf veins from Walnut Brown felt.

hearth warming

A spray of appliquéd roses puts a romantic spin on the traditional felt stocking. Hang several by the chimney with care and fill with tiny treasures for Christmas morning.

■ **Kunin Rainbow Classic Felt™: two 12" x 20" (30.5cm x 50.8cm) pieces Apple Green, one 9" x 12" (22.9cm x 30.5cm) piece each Antique White, Baby Pink, Shocking Pink and Kelly Green**

■ **Size 5 pearl cotton in baby pink, forest green and medium gold**

■ **Other supplies: scissors, disappearing-ink marker, straight pins, embroidery needle, fabric chalk**

1 Trace the pattern pieces onto the felt colors listed and cut out. Using chalk, transfer all placement lines to the right side of each felt piece.

2 Pin the toe in position on the stocking front. Secure in place along the "wavy edge" using blanket stitch and one strand of baby pink pearl cotton. Repeat this process to attach the heel. Sew on the cuff in the same manner, stitching along the top and bottom edges.

3 Pin the leaves in position, referring to diagram for placement. Secure the lower sections of the leaves using a couching stitch and one strand each of forest green (laid thread) and medium gold pearl cotton (working thread). Stitch the branches in the same manner.

4 Pin the flower bases in position. Secure in place using blanket stitch and one strand of baby pink pearl cotton.

5 Center the flower tops over the flower bases and pin in place. Using two strands of medium gold pearl cotton, secure the center of each flower with double-wrapped French knots. Using a running stitch and one strand of baby pink pearl cotton, secure the remainder of the flower top along the inner cut edge. Gently ease and reposition the curve as you stitch to give shape to the flower.

6 Pin the hanging loop sections together. Blanket-stitch along both long edges with one strand of baby pink pearl cotton. Fold in half lengthwise and secure the cut ends to the wrong side of the stocking top.

7 Pin the stocking front to the back with the wrong sides facing and the edges aligned. Blanket-stitch around the stocking with one strand of baby pink pearl cotton.

templates

Enlarge all templates 333%.

Cut two stockings from Apple Green felt.

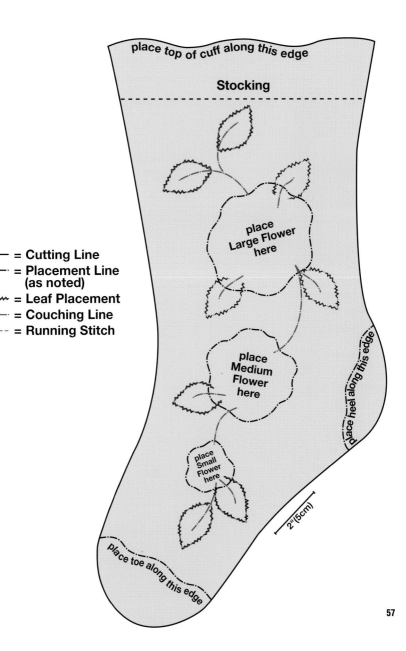

place top of cuff along this edge

Stocking

place Large Flower here

place Medium Flower here

place Small Flower here

place heel along this edge

place toe along this edge

2"(5cm)

Key

—— = Cutting Line

—·—·— = Placement Line (as noted)

〜〜〜 = Leaf Placement

—·—·— = Couching Line

------ = Running Stitch

Flower Tops

templates

Enlarge all templates 333%.

Cut one heel, one toe, two hanging loops and one cuff from Antique White felt.

Cut eight leaves from Kelly Green felt.

Cut one large, one medium and one small flower base from Shocking Pink felt.

Cut one large, one medium and one small flower top from Baby Pink felt.

Toe **Heel**

Key

──── = **Cutting Line**

─·─·─· = **Placement Line (as noted)**

∿∿∿ = **Leaf Placement**

─··─··─ = **Couching Line**

⠇⠇ = **French Knot**

----- = **Running Stitch**

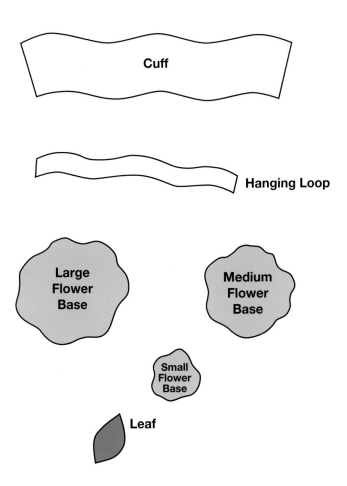

Cuff

Hanging Loop

Large Flower Base

Medium Flower Base

Small Flower Base

Leaf

- **Kunin Rainbow Plush Felt™: one 14" x 28" (35.6cm x 71.1cm) piece Denim, one 14" (35.6cm) square Cashmere Tan and two 2½" (6.4cm) squares White**

- **12" x 13" (30.5cm x 33cm) piece of ½" (1.3cm)-thick foam for insert**

- **Six-strand embroidery floss in blue and light blue**

- **Other supplies: disappearing-ink marker, scissors, straight pins, sewing machine, sewing needle, matching thread, matching heavy-duty thread, large sewing needle**

cozy toes

Slip your feet into a pair of fuzzy felt slippers. Winsome flower appliqués trimmed with blanket stitching lend a playful touch.

1 Trace four slipper tops onto the Denim felt and cut out.

2 Using the appropriate pattern size, trace two inner soles onto the Denim felt and cut out.

3 Trace two bottom soles in the same size onto the Cashmere Tan felt and cut out.

4 Using the appropriate pattern size, trace two inserts onto the foam and cut out.

5 Stitch three sides of each pair of slipper tops, with right sides together. Turn each top right side out and baste around the remaining edge to hold together.

6 Place each slipper top in position on the right side of an inner sole. Place a Cashmere Tan bottom sole onto the top and inner sole, right sides facing and pin. Sew around the edges, leaving an opening in each slipper for turning and inserting the foam lining.

7 Turn the slippers right side out, insert the foam linings and blindstitch the openings shut.

8 Trace two large flowers onto the White felt and cut out. Trace two small flowers onto the Denim felt and cut out. Using a blanket stitch and four strands of embroidery floss, outline the edges of the flower petals in a contrasting color of blue.

9 Cut two round flower centers from the Cashmere Tan felt. Using heavy thread, sew a gathering stitch around the edge of each felt circle and pull tight. Sew one flower to the toe of each slipper and hand stitch a center to each flower.

templates

**Cut two inserts
from foam.**

Foam Insert

2"(5cm)

small

medium

large

x-large

templates

**Cut four slipper tops
from Denim felt.**

**Cut two inner soles
from Denim felt.**

**Cut two sole bottoms
from Cashmere
Tan felt.**

**Cut two large flowers
from White felt.**

**Cut two small flowers
from Denim felt.**

Toe

**Sole Bottom and
Inner Sole**

2"(5cm)

Heel

small

medium

large

x-large

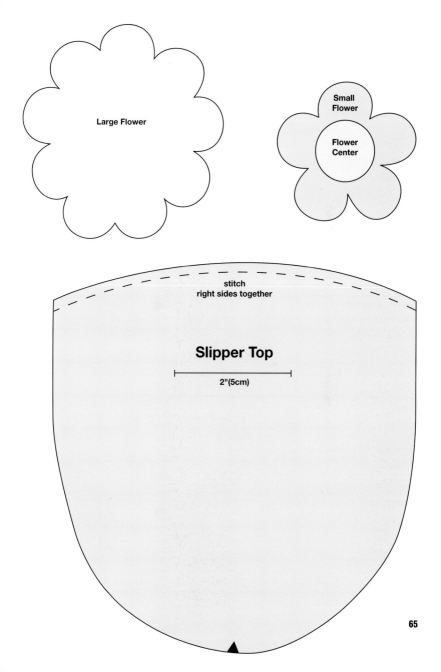

Large Flower

Small
Flower

Flower
Center

stitch
right sides together

Slipper Top

2"(5cm)

Kunin Rainbow Classic Felt™: two 9" (22.9cm) squares Royal Blue, four ½" x 9" (1.3cm x 22.9cm) strips White, one 9" (22.9cm) square each Baby Blue and Crystal Blue

24" (60cm) of ½" (1.3cm)-wide white grosgrain ribbon

Other supplies: ruler, disappearing-ink marker, scissors, straight pins, sewing machine, sewing needle, contrasting thread

templates

Cut five X's from Baby Blue felt.

Cut five O's from Crystal Blue felt.

one for the road

A felt tic-tac-toe board helps pass the time on long car trips. Double the fun by having the kids help craft one before vacation time begins.

1 Position White felt strips evenly across one Royal Blue felt square; pin and topstitch to secure.

2 Pin the two Royal Blue game board pieces together, right sides facing, and stitch around the edges, leaving an opening on one side.

3 Carefully turn the game board right side out and slipstitch the opening shut.

4 Trace five X's onto Baby Blue felt and five O's onto Crystal Blue felt; cut out the letters.

5 To transport the game board, roll it up with the X's and O's inside and tie it closed with grosgrain ribbon.

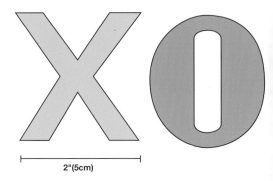

2"(5cm)

all that glitters

Heart

- Kunin Rainbow Classic Felt™: one 9" x 12" (22.9cm x 30.5cm) piece each Fuchsia and Aqua

- 40 4mm fuchsia cracked-glass beads

- 26 clear-glass seed beads

- Six-strand embroidery floss in aqua

Teardrop

- Kunin Rainbow Classic Felt™: one 9" x 12" (22.9cm x 30.5cm) piece each Grape and Shocking Pink

- Six-strand embroidery floss in purple and dark pink

- Three 6mm lavender cracked-glass beads

- 43 clear-glass seed beads

Keyhole

- Kunin Rainbow Classic Felt™: one 9" x 12" (22.9cm x 30.5cm) piece each Peacock and Lime

Sparkly sequins add shine to jewel-toned felt ornaments. Hang them on the tree or use them to dress up a holiday package.

1 Use the patterns to trace and cut out one center section and two ornament pieces from two colors of felt. Using two strands of contrasting floss, sew the center section to one ornament piece with a running stitch along the edge. (The heart ornament does not have stitching so use a few pins to hold it in place while beading.)

2 Sew beads to the center section with a beading needle and thread. Use two stitches for each bead to hold securely. (When beading teardrop and keyhole ornaments, draw the bead design first using an air-soluble pen.)

3 Pin the ornament front and back pieces together, wrong sides facing. Using two strands of contrasting floss, blanket-stitch the edges together. Before closing, lightly stuff with fiberfill.

4 For hanger, thread embroidery needle with a 12" (30.5cm)-length of silver metallic pearl cotton and make one stitch at the top of the ornament, from front to back. Thread both ends through three diamond beads; push the beads down to

the top of the ornament and tie a knot at the top of the beads. Tie a second knot about 3" (7.6cm) higher. Trim the ends and apply no-fray solution to prevent fraying.

Heart

1 Cut one inner heart from Aqua felt. Cut two outer hearts from Fuchsia felt. Sew fuchsia beads around the edge of the inner heart. Sew clear seed beads randomly over the center of the inner heart.

Teardrop

1 Cut one inner teardrop from Shocking Pink felt. Cut two outer teardrops from Grape felt. Draw three spirals on the center section as shown on the pattern. Sew clear seed beads along the lines; sew a lavender bead to the center of each spiral.

Keyhole

1 Cut one inner keyhole from Lime felt. Cut two outer keyholes from Peacock felt. Sew aqua beads in an elongated oval shape inside the edge of the center section. Sew a smaller oval of clear seed beads in the center. Sew an aqua bead at each end of the ornament; sew six clear seed beads around the aqua bead at the top only.

Six-strand embroidery floss in turquoise and green

20 4mm aqua cracked-glass beads

18 clear-glass seed beads

All ornaments

Size 5 pearl cotton in silver metallic

Three size 6/0 diamond-glass beads

Polyester fiberfill

Other supplies: scissors, straight pins, embroidery needle, beading thread, beading needle, air-soluble pen, no-fray solution

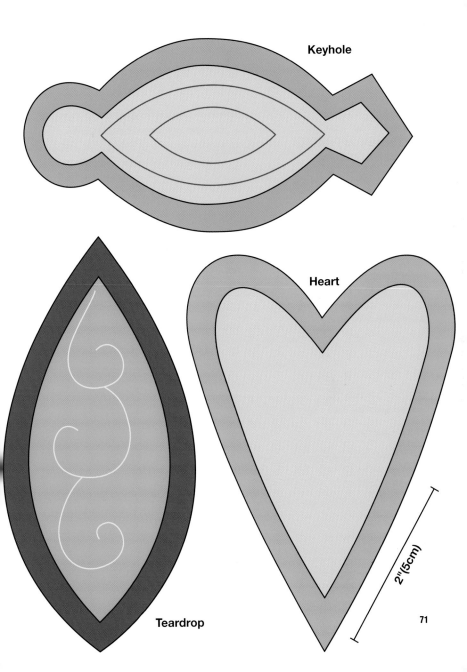

Keyhole

Heart

2"(5cm)

Teardrop

71

Silk Ribbon-Flower Coaster

- Kunin Rainbow Classic Felt™: one 9" x 12" (22.9cm x 30.5cm) piece each Fluorescent Pink and Fluorescent Green

- Fiskars® 45mm Rotary Scallop Blade

- 13" (33cm) length silk ribbon-flower trim

Beaded-Trim Coaster

- Kunin Rainbow Classic Felt™: one 9" x 12" (22.9cm x 30.5cm) piece each Shocking Pink and Peacock

- Fiskars® 45mm Rotary Wave Blade

- 13" (33cm) length beaded tube trim

Rickrack Coaster

- Kunin Rainbow Classic Felt™: one 9" x 12" (22.9cm x 30.5cm) piece each Lime and Fluorescent Orange

- Fiskars® 45mm Rotary Pinking Blade

- 14" (35.6cm) length (or more) Wrights® jumbo rickrack in Rainbow

table toppers

These cool coasters are sure to make a splash at your next get together. They're simply squares of colored felt embellished with beads, rickrack and ribbon.

1 For the center of each coaster, iron a 3" (7.6cm) square of fusible web to one side of the felt, following the manufacturer's directions. Cut out the felt to match the backing.

2 For the bottom layer, use the rotary cutter and a decorative blade to make a 4" (10.2cm) square in a contrasting color of felt.

3 Center and glue the 3"(7.6cm) square to the larger square with the backing sandwiched between the layers.

4 Use no-fray solution on the cut edges of trim where necessary. Let dry before gluing.

Silk Ribbon-Flower Coaster

1 Glue flower trim around the edge of the top layer of the coaster. Trim to size; butt ends together and glue.

- Four ⅜"to ½" (1cm to 1.3cm) assorted-color buttons

- Six-strand embroidery floss to match buttons

Grosgrain-Ribbon Coaster

- Kunin Rainbow Classic Felt™: one 9" x 12" (22.9cm x 30.5cm) piece each Gold and Fuchsia

- Fiskars® 45mm Rotary Wave Blade

- 14" (35.6cm) length of ⅜" (1cm)-wide fuchsia grosgrain ribbon

- 8" (20.3cm) length of ⅛" (.3cm)-wide gold grosgrain ribbon

- Sewing needle and matching thread (optional)

All coasters

- 3" (7.6cm)-square fusible web

- Fiskars® 45mm Rotary Cutter

- Beacon™ Fabri-Tac™ glue

- Other supplies: scissors, ruler, iron, no-fray solution

Beaded-Trim Coaster

1 Follow the directions for the Silk Ribbon-Flower Coaster, but glue the trim to the bottom layer against the edge of the top layer.

Rickrack Coaster

1 Cut the rickrack into four 2¾" (7cm) lengths. Glue each piece to one edge of the top layer of the coaster, overlapping slightly at the corners. (Note: To match colors at corners, it will be necessary to choose and cut pieces from a longer length of trim.)

2 Thread a short length of matching floss through two holes of each button with the ends on top. Tie the ends in a knot and trim to ⅜" (1cm). Use the tip of a needle to separate the strands. Glue one button onto the trim at each corner of the coaster, as pictured.

Grosgrain-Ribbon Coaster

1 To glue fuchsia ribbon to the top layer of the
coaster, work on one side at a time and glue up
to each corner. Fold the ribbon over at each
corner to form an angle and glue down the next
side. At the final corner, clip the ribbon and apply
no-fray solution.

2 Cut the gold ribbon into four equal lengths. Tie
a single knot in the center of each; trim ends at a
slant. Glue or use a needle and thread to tack a
gold knot at each corner.

picture perfect

Show off your favorite snapshot in a padded fabric frame scattered with felt violets. Easy embroidery stitches create the details on each blossom.

- **Unfinished wood frame with 5" x 7" (12.7cm x 17.8cm) opening**

- **Kunin Rainbow Classic Felt™: ½yd (.46m) Graystone and one 9" x 12" (22.9cm x 30.5cm) piece each Lavender, Orchid and Leaf Green**

- **Beacon™ Fabri-Tac™ glue**

- **Six-strand embroidery floss in purple and green**

- **Other supplies: ruler, scissors, embroidery needle, gray sewing thread, sewing needle (optional)**

1 Remove the back of the frame and the glass insert. Place the frame, front side down, on the Graystone felt. Measure and cut a felt rectangle large enough to fold over the edges and cover the back of the frame.

2 With the frame in the same position, cut the felt following the diagram and as follows: Cut one side from the outer edge to the inner edge of the frame opening. Repeat on the adjacent side, leaving a tab large enough to wrap around the corner of the frame. Repeat at the remaining corners.

3 Wrap the tabs around the corners and glue to secure. Fold the tabbed sides up over the edges and glue to the back of the frame. Repeat with the remaining two sides. If desired, use a needle and thread to sew invisible stitches to make the overlap at the corner edges as smooth as possible.

4 For the inside edges, cut a large X in the center, almost to the edge of the frame. Trim away most of the felt, but leave a margin wide enough to cover the inside edge of frame. Pull the felt up and glue to the back of the frame.

templates

Cut one frame cover from Graystone felt.

Cut four flowers from Lavender felt.

Cut three flowers from Orchid felt.

Cut seven leaves from Leaf Green felt.

Cut out circle pattern.

5 Using the patterns, trace and cut out three Orchid and four Lavender flowers. With two strands of purple floss, blanket-stitch around the edges of each flower. Cut out the circle pattern and hold it up to the center of the flower to indicate the outline of the stitches. Use floss to sew gathering stitches on the flower around the pattern edge. Pull the floss to gather the flower center; knot and clip floss. For each flower center, cut a strip of Orchid or Lavender felt about ³⁄₁₆" x 2" (.5cm x 5cm). Tie a single knot in each strip and trim ends to about ⅜" (1cm) with a slant cut. Glue or tack each strip to a flower center, using Orchid strips on Lavender flowers and Lavender strips on Orchid flowers.

6 Using the leaf pattern, trace and cut seven leaves from Leaf Green felt. With two strands of green floss, sew four fly stitches down center of each leaf. Glue each leaf, right side up, on another piece of green felt; cut out backing felt to match the leaf front.

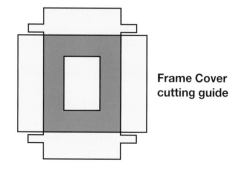

Frame Cover cutting guide

7 Arrange the flowers and leaves on the frame, clustering them at the upper righthand corner. When satisfied with the placement, glue to secure. To keep the arrangement three dimensional, apply glue only to the backs of the flower centers and the bottom edges of the leaves. Replace the frame backing and glass.

Flower Center stitching guide

2"(5cm)

Phone Book

- **Kunin Rainbow Classic Felt™: ½yd (.46m) Light Yellow, one 5" (12.7cm) square Fuchsia and remnants of Orange and Pumpkin**

- **Purchased address book**

Cat Journal

- **Kunin Rainbow Classic Felt™: ½yd (.46m) Shocking Pink, one 5" (12.7cm) square Baby Blue and remnant of Orange**

- **Purchased journal**

Both

- **Beacon™ Fabri-Tac™ glue**

- **Other supplies: disappearing-ink marker, scissors, measuring tape or ruler**

take note

Turn a simple journal and phone book into works of art by covering them in brightly colored felt and gluing on whimsical motifs. They'll be instant conversation pieces and oh-so-easy to find!

Phone Book

1 Place the open address book, cover side down, onto the Light Yellow felt and trace around it, adding 1" (2.5cm) to all sides; cut out.

2 Spread glue evenly onto the felt piece and press it onto the cover, smoothing the felt from the center to the edges and folding the excess over to the inside as if wrapping a package.

3 When the glue dries, close the book and trim the excess felt.

4 Measure the inside front and back covers of the book and cut two pieces of Light Yellow felt to these measurements. Glue the pieces to the inside covers.

5 Trace the telephone pattern onto the Fuchsia felt and cut it out. Cut the outer dial and the cord from the Orange felt and the inner dial from the Pumpkin felt.

6 Assemble the pieces as pictured and glue them to the front of the address book. Allow to dry completely before handling.

Cat Journal

1 Following steps one through four for the phone book, cover the journal in Shocking Pink felt.

Cut one telephone and one receiver from Fuchsia felt.

Cut one outer dial from Orange felt.

Cut one inner dial from Pumpkin felt.

Cut one cat from Baby Blue felt.

Cut one collar from Orange felt.

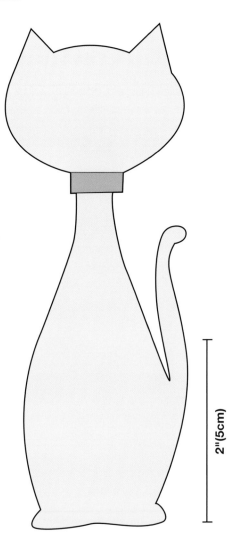

2"(5cm)

2 Trace the cat pattern onto Baby Blue felt and cut out. Trace the collar onto Orange felt and cut out.

3 Glue the cat to the journal cover. Position the collar on the cat's neck and glue in place. Allow to dry completely before handling.

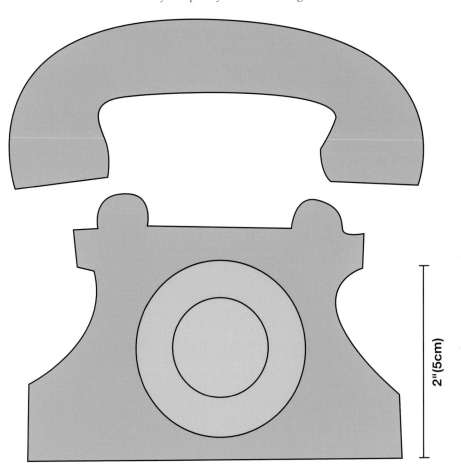

2" (5cm)

- **Kunin Rainbow Classic Felt™: 1yd (.91m) Ruby and 1yd (.91m) Sandstone**

- **½yd (.46m) paper-backed fusible web**

- **Wool yarn in ruby and sandstone**

- **Two 12" (30cm) pillow forms**

- **Circle template or pencil compass**

- **Other supplies: iron and pressing cloth, scissors, sewing machine, matching thread, straight pins, embroidery needle, ruler, pencil**

felt pillows

Add a folkloric accent to any room with throw pillows trimmed with geometric appliqués and easy embroidery stitches. Follow our red and white cream example or opt for bolder brights for a more modern look.

Square

1 Cut two 13" (32.5cm) squares from Ruby felt for the pillow front and back. Cut one 9" (22.9cm) square from Sandstone felt for the pillow top.

2 Trace one 6" (15.2cm) and one 3" (7.6cm) square onto the paper-side of the fusible web. Following the manufacturer's instructions, fuse the 6" (15.2cm) square to the wrong side of the Ruby felt and the 3" (7.6cm) square to the wrong side of the Sandstone felt. Cut out the squares. Remove the backing paper from the 6" (15.2cm) square; center and carefully fuse it to the 9" (22.9cm) square as directed. Using sandstone yarn, embroider around the edge of the 6" (15.2cm) square, alternating between cross-stitch and running stitch. Remove the backing paper from the 3" (7.6cm) square; center and carefully fuse it to the pillow front. Using ruby yarn, embroider around the edge as before.

3 Pin the 9" (22.9cm) square centered onto one 13" (32.5cm) front piece; topstitch with matching thread. Embroider around the edge of the 9" (22.9cm) square using ruby yarn.

4 Pin the appliquéd pillow top to the 13" (32.5cm) back piece, wrong sides facing. Topstitch 1" (2.5cm) from edge all around, leaving an opening on one side. Insert a pillow form and stitch opening closed. Using sandstone yarn, embroider around the edge of the pillow as before.

Circle

1 Cut two 13" (32.5cm) squares from Sandstone felt for pillow front and back. Cut one 9" (22.9cm) circle from Ruby felt for pillow top.

2 Trace one 4" (10.2cm) circle onto the paper-side of the fusible web. Following the manufacturer's instructions, fuse the web to the wrong side of the Sandstone felt. Cut out the felt circle. Remove the backing paper from the circle; center and carefully fuse it to the 9" (22.9cm) circle as directed. Thread embroidery needle with ruby

yarn and embroider the running stitch around
the inner edge of the 4" (10.2cm) circle through
both layers. Using sandstone yarn, embroider the
running stitch around the outer edge of the 4"
(10.2cm) circle through both layers.

3 Pin the 9" (22.9cm) appliquéd circle centered on
one 13" (32.5cm) front piece; topstitch ¼" (.6cm)
from the edge with matching thread. Using
sandstone yarn, embroider the running stitch
around the inner edge of the 9" (22.9cm) circle
through both layers. With ruby yarn, embroider
the running stitch around the outer edge of the
9" (22.9cm) circle through both layers.

4 Pin the appliquéd pillow top to the 13" (32.5cm)
Sandstone back piece, wrong sides facing.
Topstitch ½" (1.3cm) from the edge all around,
leaving an opening on one side. Insert a pillow
form and stitch the opening closed. Using ruby
yarn, embroider the running stitch around the
edge of the pillow through the front and back.

- **Kunin Glitter Felt™:**
  1½yds (1.38m) Purple

- **Kunin Rainbow Classic
  Felt™: four 9" x 12"
  (22.9cm x 30.5cm) pieces
  Red, three 9" x 12"
  (22.9cm x 30.5cm) pieces
  each Neon Blue, Yellow,
  Orange, Baby Blue and
  Lavender**

- **Beacon™ Fabri-Tac™
  glue**

- **Dried beans
  (for markers)**

- **Circle template or
  pencil compass**

- **Other supplies:
  ruler, scissors,
  disappearing-ink marker,
  sewing machine, sewing
  needle, sewing thread**

hop to it

**Great graphics and bold colors give an old school
favorite a hot new look. Just cut stenciled
numbers and geometric shapes from felt and glue
to a bright purple background.**

1 For the mat, cut a 3' x 4'(.92m x 1.23m) piece of
Purple felt.

2 Trace all shapes and numbers onto felt colors
listed and cut out.

3 Referring to the photo, place the numbers in the
circles and the squares and glue. Allow to dry.

4 Using the photo as a guide, evenly space the
numbers on the purple mat and glue them down.
Let dry.

5 Place the stars in a random pattern on the mat
and glue them down; let dry.

6 To make the two bean bag markers, cut two
2"(5cm) Yellow and two 2"(5cm) Red circles
from felt using the circle template. Topstitch
each pair of circles ¼"(.6cm) from edge, leaving
a 1"(2.6cm) opening. Turn right side out, fill
with beans and slipstich opening closed.

7 Using the template, cut one Red star and one
Baby Blue star from felt. Glue the stars to the
bean bag markers. Allow the markers to dry
completely before handling.

Enlarge all templates 500%.

Cut numbers from designated color felt.

Cut circles and squares from designated color felt.

Cut two stars each from Baby Blue and Red felt.

Cut one star each from Neon Blue, Yellow, Orange, Baby Blue and Lavender felt.

5

6

7

8

9

10

**Kunin Rainbow Classic
Felt™: ½yd (.46m) Crystal
Blue, one 6" x 12"
(15.2cm x 30.5cm)
piece Plum and remnants
of Aqua**

**Beacon™ Fabri-Tac™
glue**

**Other supplies:
ruler, disappearing-ink
marker, scissors, sewing
needle, matching thread**

in bloom

**Craft a cool kerchief from a triangle of blue felt.
Trimmed with big, beautiful daisies, it's
sure to turn heads. Easy-to-work blanket
stitching finishes the edges.**

1 Cut one 15" x 15" x 22" (38.1cm x 38.1cm x
55.8cm) triangle and two ½" x 12" (1.3cm x
30.5cm) ties from Crystal Blue felt.

2 Whipstitch around the edge of the triangle using
a double thickness of contrasting thread.

3 Trace the flower three times onto the Plum felt
and cut out. Trace the flower center three times
onto Aqua felt and cut out.

4 Glue the flowers onto the kerchief and the
centers onto the flowers.

5 Glue the ties to the underside of the kerchief's
side points.

Cut three flowers from Plum felt.

Cut three flower centers from Aqua felt.

2"(5cm)

Beacon Adhesives Company Inc.
125 MacQuesten Parkway South
Mount Vernon, NY 10550
914-699-3400
http://beaconcreates.com

Fiskars School, Office & Craft
7811 West Stewart Avenue
Wausau, WI 54401
800-950-0203
www.fiskars.com

Freudenberg Nonwovens
Pellon Consumer Products Division
3440 Industrial Drive
Durham, NC 27704
800-223-5275
www.pellonideas.com

Kunin Felt
P.O. Box 5000
Hampton, NH 03843-5000
800-292-7900
www.kuninfelt.com
kuninfelt@fossmfg.com

Styrofoam Brand Products
The Dow Chemical Company
P.O. Box 68
Chagrin Falls, OH 44022
440-247-4371
www.dow.com/styrofoam

felt

Editorial Director
Trisha Malcom

Editor
Colleen Mullaney

Senior Editor
Lisa Ventry

Art Director
Chi Ling Moy

Graphic Designer
Caroline Wong

Designer/Stylist
Laura Maffeo

Designers
Christina Batch
Winnie Hinish
The Design Team at Kunin Felt

Tech Editors
Pam Dailey
Michelle Lo

Copy Editor
Daryl Brower

Photography
Jack Deutsch Studios

●

Book Manager
Cara Beckerich

Production Manager
David Joinnides

**President and Publisher,
Sixth&Spring Books**
Art Joinnides